PREFACE.

The wonderful progress of Gregg's Shorthand in the past few months has created a great demand for reading matter, and this is the first of a series of books we intend to issue in the course of the next few months. The plates for the entire series were prepared and ready for the press some time ago, but most of them were lost in the fire which recently destroyed our offices. A few of the plates in this number have suffered from the flames, but we thought it best to issue the reader without further delay.

We believe that this little reader will be welcomed by both teachers and students of the system as an aid to forming an accurate style of writing. The transcript of each plate is given in typewriting with the idea of accustoming the student to correct forms.

THE GREGG PUBLISHING COMPANY.

CHICAGO, September, 1900.

Names of the States.

Names of the Principal Cities.

Names of Foreign Countries.

Wise Words.

WISE WORDS.

Have a time and place for everything and do everything in its time and place, and you will not only do more, but have far more leisure than those who are always hurrying, as if in vain attempting to regain time that had been lost.

You cannot praise a man for having done a great thing without hearing from the little man at his side who advised him to do it.

It is always a sign of poverty of mind where men are ever aiming to appear great, for they who are really great never seem to know it.

Shallow men believe in luck; strong men in cause and effect.

You will always find those men the most forward to do good, or to improve the times and manners, who are always busy.

Those who will abandon a friend for one error know but little of the human character and prove that their hearts are as cold as their judgments are weak.

You will never find time for anything. If you want time, you must make it.

If there is honor among thieves, they stole it.

An Earnest Minister.

The Quaker Woman's Sermon.

An Earnest Minister.

He was an earnest minister who, one Sunday, in the course of a sermon on the significance of little things, said: "The hand which made the mighty heavens made a grain of sand; which made the lofty mountains made a drop of water; which made you made the grass of the field; which made me made a daisy."

The Quaker Woman's Sermon.

My dear friends, there are three things I very much wonder at. The first is that children should throw stones, clubs and brickbats up into fruit trees to knock down fruit; if they would let it alone it would fall itself. The second is that men should be so foolish, and so wicked, as to go to war and kill each other; if let alone they would die themselves. And the third and last thing that I wonder at is that men should be so unwise as to go after the young women; if they would stay at home the young women would come after them.

Dear Sir:

Enclosed we send you catalogue of today's sale of grape fruit. Our trade is letting this fruit alone so far as possible. Only very few buy it, and they because they have to, as they say it is impossible for them to make any money at the present prices. Anything that was good brought a fair price.

Very truly yours,

Gentlemen:

In reply to your letter of the 10th inst. we would say that we cannot give you any reliable information regarding the parties you inquire about. We would refer you to Messrs. H. & S., of this town, who can furnish you with the information you desire.

Yours truly,

Dear Sir:

Yours of the 10th at hand, and in reply will say that we will do the best we can to get your goods along on time. As we stated to you before, the only cause of delay will be the want of cars to load at the mill and that cannot be helped. Will do the best we can to ship promptly.

Very truly yours,

Dear Sir:

We enclose a copy of our letter of January 5th. If you have not given your attention to the matter, we trust you will do so on receipt of this.

Very respectfully,

Rules for the Young Stenographer.

Rules for the Young Stenographer.

When you are called to take dictation, always spend at least five minutes looking for your note-book.

If you do not understand a word, substitute "any old thing."

If your employer is in a rush for any particular letter, always reserve that one for the last; it will make him take an interest in you.

Spend the odd moments while taking dictation chewing the eraser; it is so much cheaper than gum.

Never clean the type on your machine; it mars the uniformity of your work.

Never write on your machine when you are not compelled to, as you might increase your speed.

Never dust your machine; a layer of dirt will convince your employer that you are very busy, and he will probably raise your salary.

When you are taking dictation stop occasionally to sharpen your pencil; it will give him time to collect his thoughts.

Don't forget your chewing gum when you take dictation; it will remind him of the old home farm and the brindle cow in the shadow of the barn.

If the mail is especially heavy, take a day off; it will make your employer appreciate your services.

Gentlemen:

Your favor of April 30th was duly received, and we will forward the goods today per Merchant's Dispatch as directed.

Trusting the goods will arrive safely and meet with your approval, we remain

Yours truly,

Gentlemen:

Will you oblige me with some information regarding Messrs. B. & Co., of your town? Do they stand fair, and would you consider it safe to give them credit to the extent of four months?

Yours truly,

Dear Sir:

The check you promised us some time ago has not yet reached us. Since then several calls have been made at your office unattended with success in finding you. We have now to say that a check for the amount of our bill, $260.00, received by tomorrow will be satisfactory, and oblige

Yours truly,

Gentlemen:

We enclose your bill and bill of lading for freight shipped you today. We think you will find it a very good purchase. Hope it will please you and that we shall hear from you again. We are,

Yours truly,

Dear Sir:

We enclose check for $50.00 to settle our account for last week.

Yours truly,

Business Law In Brief.

Business Law in Brief.

Ignorance of the law excuses no one.

It is a fraud to conceal a fraud.

The law compels no one to do impossibilities.

Signatures in lead pencil are good in law.

Principals are responsible for their agents.

Agents are liable to their principals for errors.

A receipt for money is not legally conclusive.

Notes bear interest only when so stated, but do bear interest from the date of maturity.

Each individual in a partnership is liable for the whole amount of the debts of the firm.

A contract made with a minor cannot be enforced against him.

An endorser can avoid liability by writing "Without recourse" beneath his signature.

An endorsee has a right of claim against all whose names were on the bill when he received it.

Where two or more parties are jointly liable on a note, notice to one is sufficient.

Dear Sir:

We are just in receipt of the enclosed letter from John Syme. We have written him that you have charge of the matter of our claim against him, and inasmuch as we have been put to the trouble of sending an agent to Pittsburg especially to protect our claim, and will have to pay your fees for making the collection, we feel that we should not be called upon to also stand the costs of entering judgment. However, if you think it is advisable to settle with him in that way, you are authorized to do so. We have no statement of the amount of the costs. We would like you to send us a memorandum of the date of the entry and the amount of the costs incurred, which we understand the defendant is liable for.

Yours truly,

Dear Sir:

Your favor of the 17th inst. enclosing postal card from Winona Coal Co. is at hand and card is herewith returned.

In reply would say, I do not think we will be able to offer you much assistance on your coal, as at present all our cars are badly needed for our own business.

Yours truly,

Dear Sir:

I am in receipt of your letter of the 25th inst., inquiring about our train service from St. Louis to New York and Boston, and I take pleasure in informing you that our "New York and Boston Limited" train, which leaves St. Louis every evening, carries a palace sleeping car through to New York City without change, and also carries a buffet sleeping car through to Boston without change. These cars run via Niagara Falls, and are literally palaces on wheels. The time is very fast by this train.

We also take pleasure in promptly answering questions pertaining to our train service, which reaches all important points in the United States and Canada.

Yours truly,

Gentlemen:

You will, we trust, pardon the continued delay in getting to you the papers in our claim for $4.65, deducted from remittance. You will find herewith papers in full. This overcharge applies to your invoice of December 3rd, which we trust you will be able to verify.

Yours truly,

Dear Sir:

We are in receipt of your favor of the 20th inst. canceling order given our Mr. White, which we received from him under date of the 17th inst., and as you request, we cancel the order for the work. We regret, however, that you found it necessary to do this, but we never feel like crowding lumber upon our customers when they do not want it, and under the circumstances you did exactly right.

Trusting to hear from you when you are in need, we are

Yours truly,

Dear Sir:

Not having heard from you for the last week, I fear that you may not have been getting along as well as I was led to believe, and I am anxious to find how you are getting on. Do you think it will be safe for me to take a vacation for the two weeks beginning July first? While I should like to make such an arrangement, I would not feel like doing so if there was danger that you would not be able to be in the office in my absence. We have managed all right in the office up to the present time.

Yours truly,

Dear Sir:

See that none of your agents paste illustration blanks to policies. Ignorant persons might imagine that an illustration became a part of the contract by being thus attached. Under no circumstances should an illustration, or anything else not a part of the contract, be attached in any way to a policy.

Our illustration blanks are for canvassing purposes. Do not give illustrations of policies already in force, but refer all inquirers for results in such cases to us for reply.

Whenever a death claim is paid or a Tontine policy or Bond is settled, be sure to get a letter and send a copy of it to the Society. Even if the letter is merely an acknowledgment of the check, or an authorization to quote the figures, it is sufficient because we can ourselves quote the results.

When the settlement of a Tontine policy is placed in your hands, please see that it is given very prompt attention, or if anything makes it impossible for you to give it prompt attention, notify us at once.

        Yours truly,

Gentlemen:

Your letter of the 6th inst., advising me of shipment of goods, came to hand yesterday. The goods have arrived today, and I am well pleased with them.

        Yours truly,

Dear Sir:

We are in receipt of your favor with your inquiry for prices and illustrations of our work, and take pleasure in forwarding you catalogue. We are unable, however, to quote you prices direct owing to an existing contract for this year with Arnold & Bell of your city which gives them privilege of exclusive sale in Philadelphia. These parties keep a large stock of our work on hand, and will be able to supply you at a very slight advance over factory prices and at quite a saving to you in freight. If you are in the market for a supply of work, we can sell you at as low prices as can be obtained, and think our work has many special features and points of merit that you will not find in that furnished by other manufacturers. Special attention is given to the preparation of our goods for export and there will be no difficulty in your receiving them in good condition. We are just getting out a good article, which we are offering at a very low figure, and we would call your attention to that part of the catalogue which refers to them, and which we have marked for your benefit.

Yours respectfully,

Dear Sir:

Replying to yours of the 21st inst. we beg to say that your application for loan of $10,000 on your premises has been considered by our committee, and I am directed to advise you that it will be considered further if the amount can be reduced to $8,000, otherwise it is respectfully declined.

Very truly yours,

Gentlemen:

We have sold car 48961 to Messrs. Brown & Co., Philadelphia. There are four specials in this car, one of which we have instructed them to forward to destination, other three to sell for our account.

Yours truly,

Dear Sir:

In looking through some correspondence we find a letter from you dated April 17, asking that a bill be sent you for subscriptions ordered some months previous. There seemed to be no data to indicate that this letter of yours ever had attention, and further we find on our charge books a memorandum of seven subscriptions ordered by you for which we apparently have never received a remittance. Will you be kind enough to advise us whether the letter referred to was acknowledged and if payment has ever been made for these subscriptions. We enclose stamped addressed envelope for reply.

Yours respectfully,

Dear Sir:

Yours of the 23rd inst. is at hand, and in reply we beg to say that we think our charge for lengthening is quite reasonable. Should we allow forty per cent. discount from prices which are figured at net, we should be doing so at a loss. We are always glad to do anything within reason, as many of our customers will attest, but we really think it unfair that you should insist upon our furnishing goods below cost. Put yourself in the same position and you will undoubtedly agree with us.

Yours truly,

Dear Sir:

We hand you herewith statement of your account showing balance of $30.00 due for advertising. We cannot understand why you should ignore the bills, as the advertising was given in accordance with the order, and we should have had payment long before this. We should appreciate a check to cover the amount.

Yours truly,

Rough on the Congregation.

Rough on the Congregation.

---:oOo:---

The minister arose in his pulpit one Sunday morning and said, "Brethren, I have to announce that this will be my last appearance in this pulpit. I have many reasons for this. In the first place, you do not love me, because you have not paid me a dollar of my salary this year. In the second place, you do not love God, for you are doing no-nothing to advance his kingdom on earth. God does not love you, for there has not been a funeral in this parish for many months. In the third place, you do not love one another, for there has been only one wedding in two years. These being the facts, I have decided to leave this field of labor, and have accepted a position as chaplain in the jail. And now I will preach my farewell sermon from the text, I go to prepare a place for you."

---:oOo:---

Whenever there is failure, there is some superstition about luck, some step omitted, which nature never pardons.--Emerson.

Dear Sir:

Herewith I send you statement of outstanding bills against your company amounting to $473.10. You will note that some of these bills were rendered the latter part of 1897, also a number during 1898. Will you please inform me what prospect there is of having these adjusted? Anything that you can do to expedite a settlement will be appreciated by me.

Hoping to hear from you at an early date, I am

Yours truly,

Dear Sir:

The $10.00 received from you has been disposed of, as per receipts enclosed for $9.00, which leaves $1.00 still in my hands to your credit. As this is not enough to pay one assessment, I thought I would inform you, so that you could make another remittance previous to November 20th, as there is likely to be another one due.

Yours truly,

Gentlemen:

The changes of our office when our agency for your company was discontinued forced us to let out some of our help.

Among these was a young man who has been with us for some time, and whom we think would be a good man to drum up trade in Chicago, or in fact after a little experience, anywhere.

We should like to know if you think it would be advisable to put a man on in Chicago either on salary or commission. We paid forty cents per case commission last summer, but in our opinion it would be better to pay at least a small salary, as our experience at that time showed that it was very hard for a man to make anything on a commission basis.

Please write us about this as soon as possible, and oblige

Yours truly,

Dear Sir:

In regard to the interest on the deposits belonging to the J. R. Miller estate, I would say that I consider the following proposition would be fair to the estate as well as to yourself, namely, two per cent on average monthly deposits, to be paid on the first of each and every month for the period during which the deposit remains, interest to be computed and remitted for the months of December and January as well as the present and future months.

This arrangement has been agreed to by the First National Bank of Cleveland, with whom I have also made deposits in the name of the estate and it is entirely satisfactory to them, as I trust it will be to you.

Inasmuch as I have made this arrangement with the First National Bank, and as you and I had previously agreed to let this interest negotiation rest for a short time, I would now consider it a favor if you would consent to the same arrangement as that made with the First National Bank, as I, of course, naturally desire to have the interest at both banks on a uniform basis.

Yours respectfully,

Gentlemen:

Your wire received this morning. We are sending you today, under separate cover, list of cars in transit unsold, and if you can use any of them, please wire us immediately on receipt of this letter, as we offer them subject to being unsold.

Hoping you will see something attractive to you, we are

Very truly yours.

Dear Sir:

We have your letter of October 21st enclosing $5.00 for supplies. We have entered your order for careful attention and will make shipment promptly.

Thanking you for the order, we are

Yours truly.

Dear Sir:

We are in receipt of your favor of the 2nd inst. requesting particulars in regard to our method of doing business. In reply we wish to say that we are desirous of securing agents for the sale of our line of custom made clothing. We ship all goods on a C. O. D. basis, subject to examination, but we require a small deposit of one dollar on each order. If the goods are not exactly as represented, or do not fit your customer, you are not obliged to accept the same, and we then refund the deposit paid on the order. Our reason for requiring a deposit is to protect ourselves and our agents from irresponsible persons when they are not required to pay a deposit, and have no idea where they are to get the money to pay for the goods on arrival. If you are of the opinion that you will be able to do any business for us, we will be pleased to send you our sample line at once.

Awaiting your reply, we remain

Yours truly,

Dear Sir:

We are in receipt of your favor of the 30th ult. making application for an agency in your locality. As we are not represented, we are pleased to state that we will appoint you our agent, and send you our sample line immediately. You will find full instructions, order blanks, etc., with the sample. We have no doubt you will be able to do considerable business for us.

Wishing you success, and hoping to hear from you at an early date, we remain

Yours truly,

Advertisement of a Law Book.

Advertisement of a Law Book.
---:oOo:---

  The plan and aim of this book, as expressed in the preface, is "to bring the leading and essential principles of the law of personal property within a narrow compass, and in such a manner as to furnish the student with the means of acquiring an adequate and discriminating knowledge of the subject without unnecessary and confusing discussion, and the practitioner with a ready and reliable solution of questions arising in the exigencies of his professional business, when time is wanting for extended research.

  Great care has been taken to formulate definitions with reliable accuracy, and to state principles clearly and concisely, presenting the law as it is without profitless and wearisome discussion as to what it ought to be. All classes and species of personal property are discussed with more or less fullness, and subjects are treated analytically in logical order, thus enabling the reader to readily find what he seeks without losing his time or way in a vexatious and often useless search.

---:oOo:---

"Keep On."

"KEEP ON."

In writing from dictation it should be an invariable rule never to allow one's self to pause when a difficult or doubtful word or phrase is encountered. It should be understood that whenever the rate of dictation (whatever it may be) has been settled, the reader shall mercilessly proceed at that rate, and shall be no more indulgent of the writer's occasional slowness than an actual speaker would be. Nothing can more surely lead to a sluggish mental process, or more surely delay the acquisition of speed, than for the writer to indulge the habit of pausing and pondering upon every uncommon word, or what is still worse, suspending the dictation in order that his doubts as to an outline may be settled by reference to a dictionary or a text-book. "Keep on" should be the inflexible rule for writer and reader. The writer should be able to get down the difficult words somehow, but if not, better a hundred times that there should be an absolute hiatus in his notes than that he should be humored by allowing him to pause and ponder-- a habit, which, if indulged, must disappoint the hope of ever becoming a rapid writer. Pausing and pondering upon hard words, while the

dictation is accommodatingly retarded or suspended, will never teach one how to write such words when the speaking goes right on.

Unless the regular rate of dictation is somewhat retarded (as it should not be) when a hard word is encountered the young writer, while tackling the difficulty, will necessarily fall somewhat behind, as even the most accomplished reporter will often do in a similar situation. It is desirable, then, that speed practice should train the young stenographer to write, when necessary, a number of words behind the speaker. A prominent business educator has said: "There is one practice which we enforce in the study of shorthand that would be valuable to anybody, and that is the habit of fixing long sentences in the mind, so as to recall them automatically. A reporter who can do this has almost any speaker at his command, for while the speaker stops for breath or to collect his thoughts for a new start, the pen of the ready writer, through the aid of a trained memory, is bringing up the rear."--From "The Factors of Shorthand Speed," by David Wolfe Brown.

Made in the USA
Middletown, DE
04 December 2024